# MAGNETISM

## experimenting with science

Antonella Meiani

⌐ Lerner Publications Company • Minneapolis

First American edition published in 2003 by Lerner Publications Company

Published by arrangement with Istituto Geografico DeAgostini, Novara, Italy

Originally published as *Il Grande Libro degli Esperimenti*

Copyright © 1999 by Istituto Geografico DeAgostini, Novara, Italy

Translated from the Italian by Maureen Spurgeon.
Translation copyright © 2000 by Brown Watson, England.

All rights reserved. International copyright secured. No part of this book may be reproduced, stored in a retrieval system, or transmitted in any form or by any means—electronic, mechanical, photocopying, recording, or otherwise—without the prior written permission of Lerner Publications Company, except for the inclusion of brief quotations in an acknowledged review.

This book has been adapted from a single-volume work entitled *Il Grande Libro degli Esperimenti*, originally published by Istituto Geografico DeAgostini, Novara, Italy, in 1999. New back matter was developed by Lerner Publications Company.

Lerner Publications Company
A division of Lerner Publishing Group
241 First Avenue North
Minneapolis, MN 55401 U.S.A.

Website address: www.lernerbooks.com


Library of Congress Cataloging-in-Publication Data

Meiani, Antonella.
    [Il Grande libro degli esperimenti. English. Selections]
    Magnetism / by Antonella Meiani ; [translated from the Italian by Maureen Spurgeon].—
  1st American ed.
      p.   cm. — (Experimenting with science)
    Includes bibliographical references and index.
    Summary: Describes a variety of experiments that explore the world of magnets and magnetism, arranged in the categories "Magnets," "Magnetic Poles," "Magnetic Force," and "Magnetism and Electricity."
    ISBN: 0–8225–0085–X (lib. bdg. : alk. paper)
    1. Magnetism—Experiments—Juvenile literature. [1. Magnetism—Experiments.
  2. Experiments.]  I. Title.
QC753.8.M4513  2003
538'.078—dc21                             2001050464

Manufactured in the United States of America
1 2 3 4 5 6 – JR – 08 07 06 05 04 03

# Table of Contents

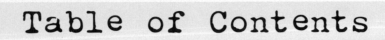

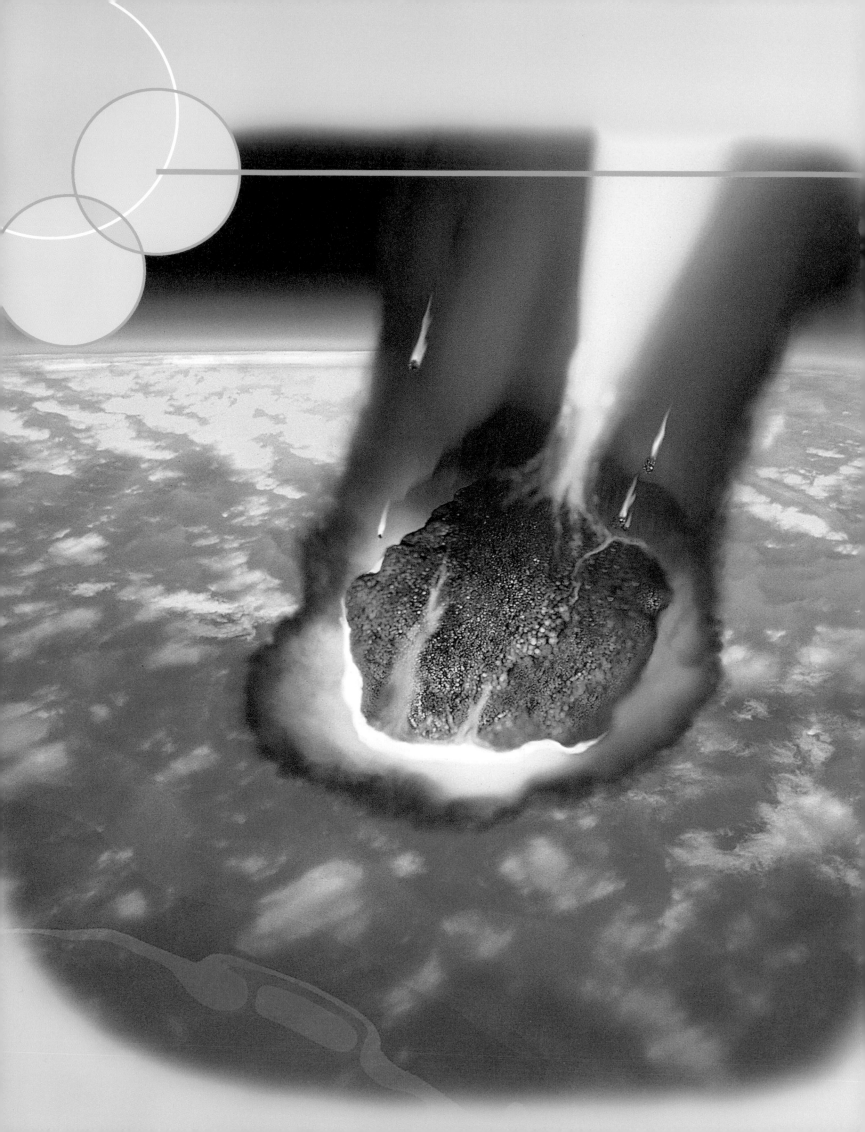

# Magnetism

Can a magnet attract anything? What makes a compass's needle move? Can an object be magnetized? How is an electromagnet made? You will find the answers to these and many other questions by doing the experiments in the following pages, in the following sections:

- Magnets
- The magnetic poles
- Magnetic force
- Magnetism and electricity

# Magnets

The power of magnets to attract steel objects and to attach themselves to metal surfaces has fascinated people for hundreds of years. To understand this power, we must first study the structure and the characteristics of magnets. In the following pages we put large and small magnets to the test and discover how to block their force, as well as using magnets to make toys and games. All the experiments are safe to do, but an adult must be on hand to use some of the tools that are required.

# Can magnets attract anything?

## WHAT CAN RESIST ATTRACTION?

### You need:
- things made of different materials: iron, wood, glass, plastic, steel, fabric, paper
- different surfaces: the door of a refrigerator, the door of a closet, a wall, a window pane, . . .
- magnet tied to a thread

### What to do:

1 Divide the objects into two groups: metal and nonmetal.

2 Hold the magnet close to the objects in the first group, one at a time.

3 Now do the same with the objects in the second group.

4 Hold the magnet close to the surface of the refrigerator, the closet door, the wall, and the window.

### What happens?
Some metal objects attach themselves to the magnet. Others do not. The nonmetal objects are not attracted. The magnet is attracted to some surfaces, but not to others.

### Why?
Magnets are pieces of steel or iron that have a special ability to attract objects made from steel, iron, nickel, cobalt, chromium, or materials that contain a small amount of any of these metals. Wood, glass, plastic, paper, and fabrics are not drawn by the force of the magnet. The force of attraction between the magnet and a large steel surface makes the magnet move towards the surface, because the magnet weighs less than the surface.

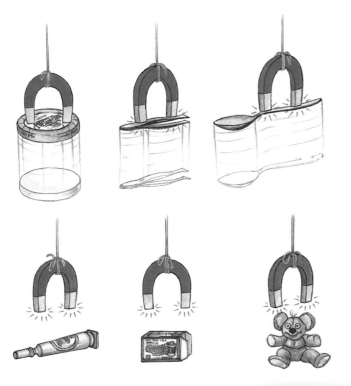

## The discovery of magnetism

More than two thousand years ago, the ancient Greeks discovered a mineral that was able to attract iron. This mineral is magnetite (magnetic iron ore). Magnetite gets its name from the ancient city of Magnesia (today called Manisa in Turkey) where it was found.
Fragments of magnetite are called natural magnetite. Today, magnets can be made from pieces of iron or steel by using a special process called magnetization.

# Magnets exert their power of attraction on objects of iron, steel, and certain other metals.

# Can magnets work through substances?

## UNDERWATER MAGNETISM

### You need:
- magnet
- pitcher
- paper clip
- water

### What to do:

1 Pour water into the pitcher and drop in the paper clip. Then invite a friend to take the paper clip out, but without putting a hand in the water.

2 Place the magnet on the outside of the pitcher, near the paper clip. When the paper clip moves towards the magnet, draw the magnet slowly up towards the top.

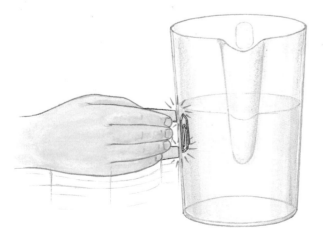

### What happens?
The paper clip follows the movement of the magnet until it is above the level of the water. In this way, it is possible to take it out without getting your hand wet!

### Why?
The force of the magnet also works through the pitcher of water. If the sides of the pitcher were iron or steel, the paper clip would still be drawn to the magnet, but with less intensity because part of the magnetic force would be absorbed by the sides of the pitcher.

## Magnets under water

Because they can also exert their power under water, magnets are widely used during underwater construction and repair work. For example, engineers use magnets to hold instruments and equipment in a safe place, and for holding parts in position during work.

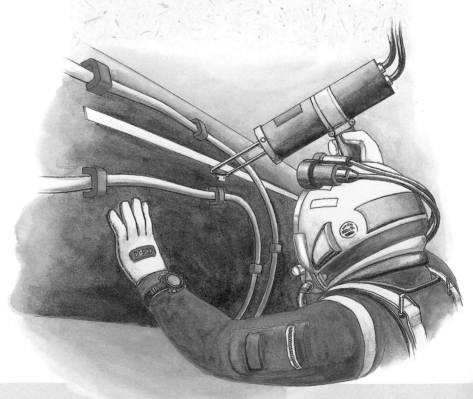

# A SET COURSE

## You need:
- thin cardboard
- scissors
- tape
- felt-tipped pens
- large piece of strong cardboard
- two little sticks
- two magnets
- two large steel washers
- four thick books
- table

## What to do:

1 Draw four rectangles with rounded corners and cut them out. Draw the top view of a car on two of the shapes and color them in.

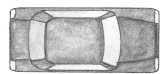

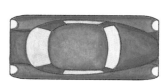

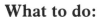

2 Tape each washer between a plain shape and a decorated one.

3 Draw two courses on the strong cardboard, each with a start and a finish. Color them in. Then place the cardboard on the books, as shown in the picture.

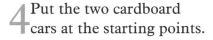

4 Put the two cardboard cars at the starting points.

5 Tape a magnet to each stick.

6 Position the stick magnets underneath the cardboard, under the two cars, so that you can use the magnets to move the cars along the courses. Then ask a friend to have a race with you.

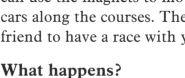

## What happens?
The cars move along the course, following the magnets that are under the cardboard.

## Why?
The force of the magnet passes through the cardboard and attracts the washers taped inside the cars. So the cars go along, following the movement of the magnets.

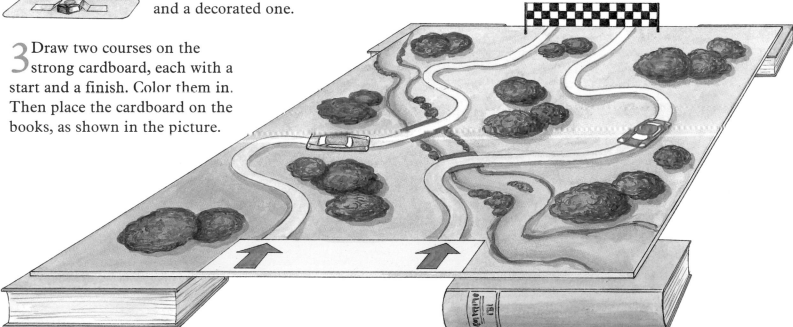

Magnetic force can pass through objects and substances.

# Can magnets work at a distance?

## MAGNETIC BOAT RACE

**You need:**
- two sticks, each about 40 cm (15 in.) long
- two magnets
- two pieces of string, each about 30 cm (12 in.) long
- four needles
- colored cardboard
- scissors
- six corks
- toothpicks
- tape
- large bowl
- water

**What to do:**

1 To make a fishing rod, tie one end of a string to the end of a stick and the other end to a magnet. Make a second fishing rod in the same way.

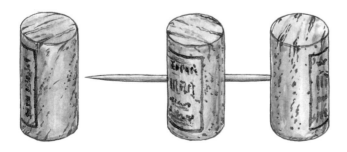

2 To make a fishing boat, first take three corks and link them together with a toothpick, as shown in the picture.

3 Stick two needles into the center cork to make the ship's masts. For the sails, cut squares from the cardboard and tape them to the needles.

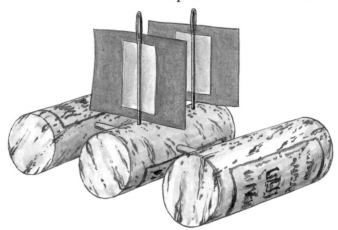

4 Fill the bowl with water and launch the boats. Hold your fishing rod above one of the boats and invite a friend to hold the other fishing rod.

**What happens?**
The movement of the fishing rods above the bowl makes the boats move, even though the magnets never touch the boats.

**Why?**
The force of the magnets draws the needles, even at a distance, and this guides the movement of the boats.

## COMPARE THE FORCE

**You need:**
- three magnets of different sizes
- some objects made of iron, steel, or nickel (coins, for example)
- table
- ruler

**What to do:**

1 Place the magnets on the table in a row, about 10 cm (4 in.) apart.

2 Place some metal objects in a row on the table. This row should be parallel to the row of magnets, but some distance from it.

3 Using the ruler, gradually push the metal objects closer and closer to the magnets.

**What happens?**
Some of the coins are attracted by the magnets almost at once, others only when they are a short distance away.

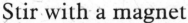

**Why?**
Magnets can exert their force at a distance from things. The larger the magnet, the stronger its force and the greater the distance at which it can attract objects.

## Stir with a magnet

Because they can exert their force at a distance and through substances, magnets can be used for medical research. In chemical laboratories, it is often necessary to mix substances in tiny quantities, without these coming into contact with any other materials. This is done by placing a tiny metal plate with a sterile covering in the bottom of a test tube, and a magnet underneath the test tube. When the substances have been put in the test tube, the magnet is made to turn at a set speed. The magnet turns the plate inside the test tube and so mixes the substances. (These pieces of equipment are called agitators.)

**A magnet can exert its force even at a considerable distance if it is powerful enough.**

# What can block the force of a magnet?

## TRAP THE MAGNETIC FORCE

### You need:
- some sheets of newspaper
- pieces of aluminum foil
- scraps of fabric
- some foam rubber
- large magnet
- something made of iron or steel

### What to do:
1 Wrap the magnet in a sheet of newspaper. Then try to attract the iron object.

2 Do the same thing with the other materials.

3 Now wrap each magnet in a second layer of the same material. Add more layers, until the force of the magnet weakens and then stops.

### What happens?
The magnet attracts the object through one thin layer of material. But as the thickness of layers increases, it can no longer exert its force.

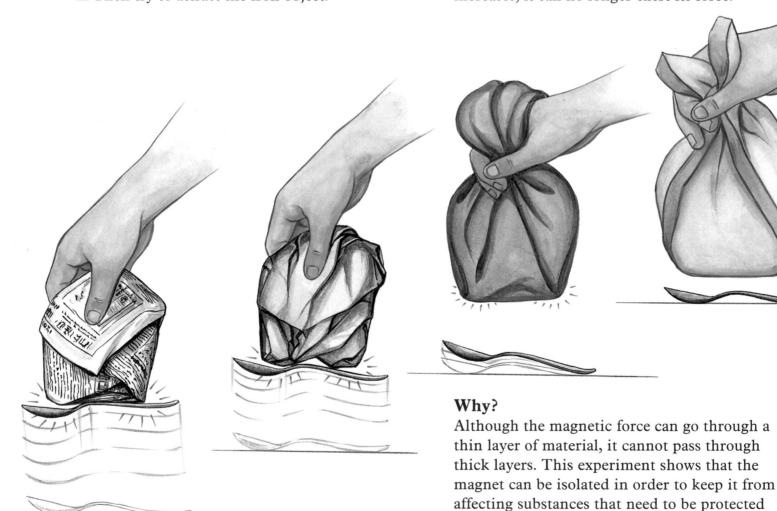

### Why?
Although the magnetic force can go through a thin layer of material, it cannot pass through thick layers. This experiment shows that the magnet can be isolated in order to keep it from affecting substances that need to be protected from magnetic attraction.

## The force of a magnet can be neutralized by a thick layer of non-magnetic material.

# What does the power of a magnet depend on?

## A TEST OF POWER

### You need:
- magnets of different shapes (horseshoe, bar, round) and different sizes
- things made of iron or steel (paper clips, coins, nails)
- cardboard boxes

### What to do:
1 Sort the metal objects into boxes.

2 Hold each magnet over each box in turn and count how many of each kind of object are drawn to it.

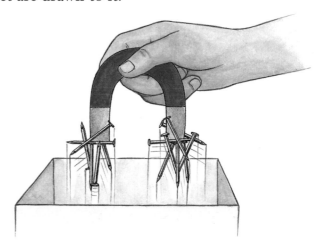

### What happens?
Some magnets attract more objects than others.

### Why?
The shape and size of a magnet influence its power. An iron horseshoe magnet is more powerful than a bar magnet, which, in turn, is more powerful than a round magnet. With magnets of the same shape, the larger the magnet, the more powerful it is.

## Tiny magnets on tape

The tape used in a cassette player is magnetic tape. It is covered in metal oxide that can easily be magnetized. Patterns of varying magnetic fields on the tape pass the recording head in the machine. The recording head is made of a magnet powered by electricity. This changes the magnetization of the tape in a certain way so that, as the tape passes the playback head, the magnetic patterns become translated into electronic signals that are transformed into sound through a speaker.

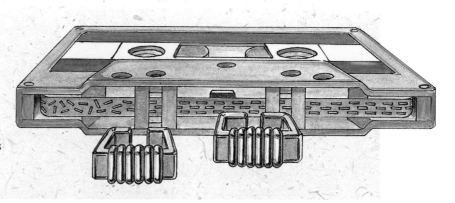

## The strength of a magnet is linked to its shape and its size.

# The magnetic poles

Have you ever tried to beat the invisible strength of two magnets that are attracted to each other? It is hard to do! In the next pages you can find out why this is so, and discover that the largest magnet of all is right under your feet. . . . It is Earth, which, just like any other magnet, has its own magnetic poles. These poles determine the direction all compass needles point, and they cause the spectacular aurora borealis (northern lights).

# Date Due Receipt

02/28/2017

## Items checked out to

patron name

TITLE        The magnet book / Shar...
BARCODE      3061300923366
DUE          03-21-17 00:00AM

TITLE        The science book of gravity ?...
BARCODE      3061300868487
DUE          03-21-17 00:00AM

TITLE        Cool gravity activities : fun...
BARCODE      3061300902983
DUE          03-21-17 00:00AM

TITLE        Magnets to generators ?...
BARCODE      3061300953382
DUE          03-21-17 00:00AM

TITLE        Experiments with magnets ?...
BARCODE      3061300264800
DUE          03-21-17 00:00AM

TITLE        Magnetism / Anthony...
BARCODE      3061300151757
DUE          03-21-17 00:00...

# Date Due Receipt

02/28/2017

Items checked out to

Leo-Carney, Jennifer

TITLE       The magnet book / Shar
BARCODE        30613000923866
DUE            03-21-17 00:00AM

TITLE The science book of gravity /
BARCODE        30613000866487
DUE            03-21-17 00:00AM

TITLE     Cool gravity activities : fun
BARCODE      3 0613 00190 7983
DUE            03-21-17 00:00AM

TITLE       Magnets to generators /
BARCODE        30613000593362
DUE            03-21-17 00:00AM

TITLE  Experiments with magnets /
BARCODE        30613002654600
DUE            03-21-17 00:00AM

TITLE       Magnetism / Antonella
BARCODE        3061300157578
DUE            03-21-17 00:00A

# Do all parts of a magnet have the same force?

## LINES OF POWER

**You need:**
- iron filings (obtainable from a workshop, or by filing a piece of iron)
- bar magnet
- horseshoe magnet
- two postcards

**What to do:**

1 Place one postcard on the bar magnet.

2 Sprinkle the iron filings on the card. Give the edge of the card a few taps with your finger.

3 Now do the same with the horseshoe magnet.

**What happens?**
Most of the iron filings are centered around the outside of the magnet. A smaller amount is scattered around.

**Why?**
The magnetic force of a magnet is concentrated at the poles, meaning the ends of the magnet. Away from the poles, the magnetism is not as strong.

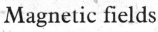

## Magnetic fields

Iron filings placed around a magnet arrange themselves according to the lines of force that show us the area in which magnetism is active. This area is called a magnetic field. The objects attracted by the magnet are drawn inside this magnetic field. The magnetic forces are distributed around the magnet in a set way. With the filings in the last experiment, we saw this only in a horizontal plane. The same force also works on a vertical plane.

**The magnetism exerted by a magnet is more intense at its ends, which we call the magnetic poles.**

# Why do two magnets sometimes repel (push apart)?

## FLOATING MAGNETS

**You need:**
- two bar magnets
- red, blue, and transparent tape
- compass
- two cardboard boxes of the same size
- scissors
- two pencils
- string

**What to do:**

1 Tie a magnet onto a piece of string, as shown in the picture. Hold it over the compass until the compass needle stops spinning. Then compare the position of the magnet with the needle of the compass. Put a little piece of red tape on the pole the needle points towards, and blue tape on the opposite pole. Now do the same with the other magnet.

2 Bring the two poles of the same color close together. Then do the same with poles of a different color.

**What happens?**
The poles of the same color are repelled. Poles of the opposite color are attracted.

3 Tape a magnet inside each box. Close the box. On the outside, put pieces of blue and red tape on the boxes to match the two poles of the magnet inside.

4 Place the two pencils on one of the boxes. Put the second box on top of the pencils, so its tape colors match those of the first box.

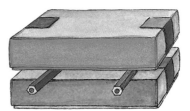

5 Wrap the clear tape around the two boxes. Then take out the two pencils. Press down on the upper box.

**What happens?**
The upper box floats above the one underneath.

**Why?**
The two poles of each magnet have opposite magnetic changes (negative and positive). The charges of opposite poles attract. The charges of the same poles repel (push apart). Because the poles were lined up the same way, each box pushed the other away. You managed to beat this force of repulsion between them by pushing down. Once you let go, the upper box returned to its original position.

## PUSH AT A DISTANCE

### You need:
- two bar magnets with opposite poles marked (see last experiment)
- toy truck
- tape

### What to do:
1 Tape one bar magnet on the truck.

2 Use the other magnet to push and pull the truck without touching it.

### What happens?
When you bring the same poles together, you push the truck away. When you bring different poles together, you bring the truck towards you.

### Why?
The truck moves because of the magnetic force between the two magnets. The truck moves towards the magnet that you have in your hand (two different poles attract each other) or away from it (two poles of the same charge repel each other). You can use this experiment to play games with your friends.

## Trains without wheels

Some high-speed trains have no wheels. Instead, there are magnets on the track and on the train, roughly where the wheels would be. These magnets are powered by electricity and arranged so that the same magnetic poles are aimed at one another. As the magnets repel, the train floats above the track. These trains move without any friction. Because of this, they can go very fast.

## The opposite poles of two magnets attract each other. The same poles repel each other.

# What makes the needle of a compass move?

## TO FIND NORTH

**You need:**
- large bowl
- water
- bar magnet with opposite poles marked (see p. 16)
- flat Styrofoam tray (smaller than the bowl—it must be able to move on the surface of the water without hitting the sides of the bowl)
- red and blue tape

Before starting, check that there are no items made of steel or iron within reach.

**What to do:**

1 Tape the magnet to the center of the Styrofoam tray. Fill the bowl with water and float the Styrofoam tray on the surface of the water.

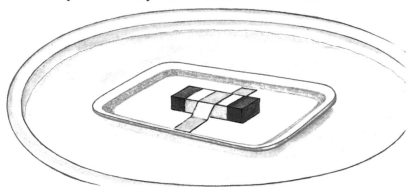

2 Spin the tray around. Wait until it stops moving.

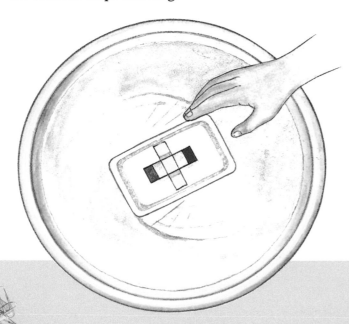

3 Put red and blue tape on the edge of the bowl to match the two poles of the magnet.

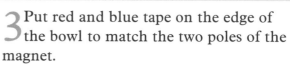
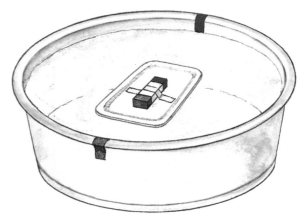

4 Now spin the tray again.

**What happens?**
When the tray stops, the poles of the magnet once again match the two marks on the bowl.

**Why?**
The magnetic force exerted by Earth is so strong that it makes all movable magnets point one pole towards the North Pole, and the other towards the South Pole.

## Earth's magnetism

Earth acts like a great big magnet. It produces a magnetic field that makes compass needles and magnets point in the direction of its magnetic poles. It is believed that this phenomenon is due both to the composition of Earth's core, which is made of iron and nickel, and Earth's rotation.

The lines that mark out Earth's magnetic field go from one pole to the other. The needle of a compass follows these lines. Earth's magnetic north pole is not the same as the geographic North Pole that we see on the map. The magnetic north pole is on the island of Bathurst in Canada, 1,900 kilometers (1,200 mi.) from the geographic North Pole. The magnetic south pole is located at a point in the sea 2,600 kilometers (1,600 mi.) from the geographic South Pole. These magnetic poles are not fixed. They change their position, although these changes take place over thousands of years.

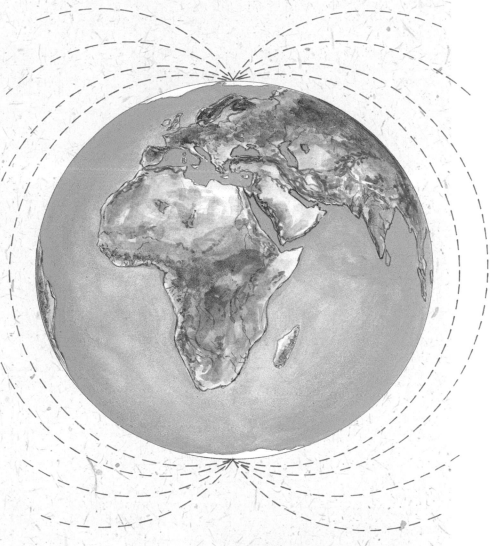

## The compass

The first to make use of Earth's magnetism to find their way around were the Chinese. They floated a little table with a bar of magnetite on it on water and watched how it moved. The first compasses began to be used in Europe in A.D. 1200, perhaps introduced by the Arabs. There are different types of compasses, but the best known is the magnetic compass. The magnetic needle is placed at the center of the compass's face on a pivot, so that it can rotate. The needle positions itself in the north/south direction due to Earth's magnetic field, and so it indicates the four cardinal points (north, south, east, and west), as well as directions in between (northeast, southwest, etc.). The cardinal points and other directions are shown on the face of the compass, with the colored tip of the needle always pointing north.

Earth acts like an enormous magnet. It attracts any magnetic needle that is free to move.

# Magnetic force

Now we will discover something else about the mysterious force generated by magnets. In this section you will be able to experiment with a magnetic object that in turn can become capable of attracting other objects. Then you will discover how it is possible to give a needle or a nail a magnetic force and how we can make it lose this force. You will see what happens when a magnet is broken in half, and finally, how we can use magnetic force to play at beating the force of gravity.

# Can something be made magnetic?

## MAKE A MAGNET

### You need:
- bar magnet
- two large needles

### What to do:
**1** Using one end of the magnet, stroke each needle along its entire length 40 times, each time in the same direction.

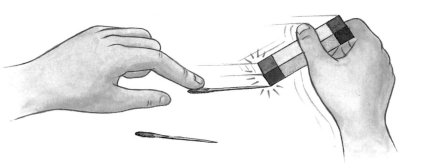

**2** Push one needle close to the other, first pushing with the point, then with the eye of the needle.

### What happens?
The needles either attract or repel, depending on the end that you push forward.

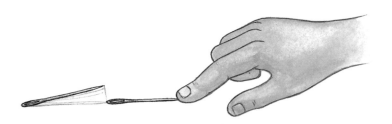

### Why?
Rubbing the magnet on the needles has created a permanent magnetization. The needles are, in fact, acting like two magnets. They attract or repel one another, depending on which poles you bring together.

## Making magnets

People have learned not only to use natural magnets, but also to make artificial magnets from iron or other special materials. The materials used to make artificial magnets are subjected to heat and then left to cool in molds in the presence of a strong magnetic field. Once cooled and hardened, the material will have acquired magnetic properties.

## Watches and magnets

Bringing a magnet near a steel watch that has a spring is dangerous. The force of the magnet may magnetize the steel parts permanently. This means that the parts will no longer be able to move correctly and the watch will not work.

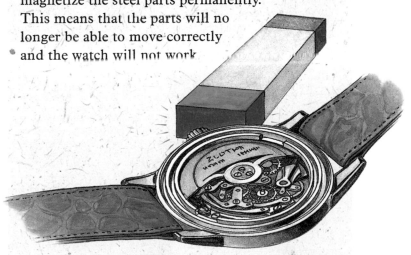

An object made of iron or steel can be magnetized by stroking it with one end of a magnet.

# Can a magnet lose its force?

## TO ATTRACT OR NOT TO ATTRACT

**You need:**
- some needles
- magnet
- hard surface

**What to do:**

1 Stroke a needle along its entire length using one end of the magnet. Stroke in the same direction 40 times.

2 Bring the magnetized needle near to the other needles.

**What happens?**
As in the last experiment, the magnetized needle attracts the others.

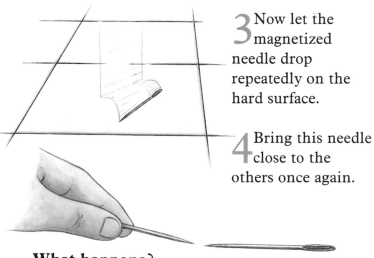

3 Now let the magnetized needle drop repeatedly on the hard surface.

4 Bring this needle close to the others once again.

**What happens?**
The magnetized needle no longer attracts the others.

**Why?**
The needle has lost its magnetic force as a result of being dropped on the hard surface. Stroking the needle magnetizes it by lining up the particles that make up the needle. With each drop, the particles are shaken around. This puts the particles in a muddle. The result is a loss of the magnetic power.

## How an object is magnetized

The inside of a metal object is subdivided into tiny little sectors called domains. Normally these are positioned in many different ways and their magnetic forces are cancelled out. The stroking of a magnet lines them all up so that the object becomes a magnet. But if a magnet is dropped repeatedly, the domains become disarranged, and the magnetic force ceases.

# When magnets are dropped or subjected to knocks, they can become demagnetized.

# Can a magnet have only one pole?

## DIVIDE UP THE MAGNETIC FORCE

### You need:
- big needle that is okay to break
- bar magnet
- two pairs of pliers
- pins

### What to do:

1 Magnetize the needle, as in the last few experiments.

2 Bring one end of the magnet close to each of the two ends of the needle. One end of the needle will be attracted. The other end will be repelled.

3 Ask an adult to use the pliers to break the needle in half.

4 Bring one end of the magnet near to each end of each of the two pieces of the needle.

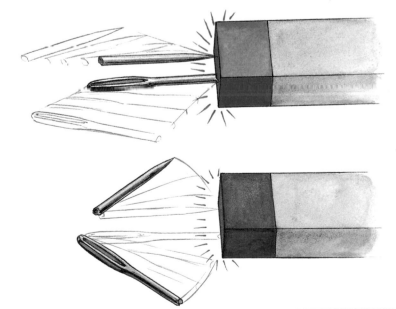

### What happens?
The two parts of the needle both act like small magnets, each with a north and a south pole.

5 Break each piece of the needle in half once again. Bring the magnet close to each piece. Then hold the pieces of needle near the pins.

### What happens?
All the pieces of the needle are attracted or repelled by the two poles of the magnet and they all attract the pins. So the pieces of the needle are now small magnets, each with two poles.

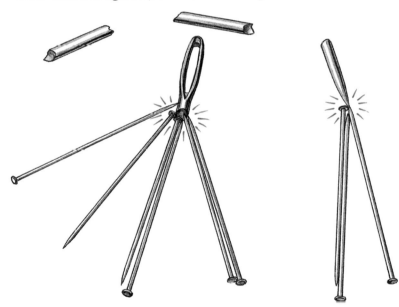

### Why?
Magnets are made up of countless tiny magnets called magnetic elements, each one with a positive pole and a negative pole. If we divide the magnet into little pieces, each piece will still have two distinct poles. From this experiment, you will see that magnetism is present in each atom (the tiniest part) of a magnet.

# A magnet's negative and positive charges are always at the two opposite ends.

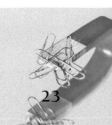

# Can magnetism be transmitted?

## THE MAGNETIC CHAIN

### You need:
- magnet
- two nails

### What to do:

1 Pick up one nail with the magnet. Then pull this nail towards the second one.

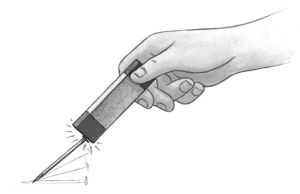

### What happens?
The first nail attracts the second one.

2 Take the first nail off the magnet, but keep the magnet close by.

### What happens?
Once again, the first nail attracts the second. The two nails remain linked.

3 Move the magnet away.

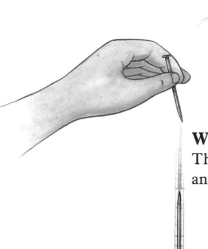

### What happens?
The two nails separate and the second one falls.

### Why?
On contact with the magnet, the first nail is magnetized and works like a magnet on the second nail. The magnetic force of the magnet is also exerted nearby, and so this force is transmitted to the two nails in both parts of the experiment. This transmission is then broken when the magnet is moved away.

## EXCHANGE OF MAGNETISM

### You need:
- nail
- bar magnet
- steel ball (like the ones found inside a ball bearing)

### What to do:
1 Bring the magnet close to the steel ball. Touch the ball with your finger to test the force by which it is drawn to the magnet.

2 Touch the nail to the ball, then pull it away.

### What happens?
The ball attaches itself to the nail.

### Why?
The magnetic force of the magnet passes through the ball and into the nail, giving it the same magnetic force.

# Magnetic Induction

In the picture below, a card has been sprinkled with iron filings, so that you can see magnetization by induction (magnetic force transmitted without contact) of a key that is near a magnet. Around the key, which is made of iron, a second magnetic field has formed. Iron, like cobalt, nickel, and steel, is a ferromagnetic material. The domains of ferromagnetic materials are composed of magnetic elements. When they are subjected to a magnetic field, the object is transformed into a magnet. But other substances, like air or water, have a low level of magnetism. When these substances are subjected to a magnetic field, they do not become magnetized. Substances that are weakly pulled towards a strong magnet are called paramagnetic. Substances that are weakly repelled by a magnet are called diamagnetic.

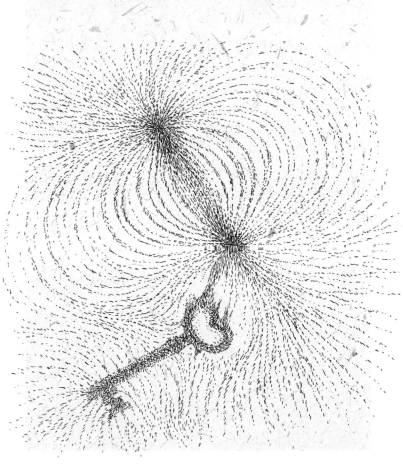

# Magnetism can be transmitted temporarily by contact or by induction.

# Can magnetic force cancel out gravity?

## THE KITE

**You need:**
- magnet tied to a thread
- paper clip
- colored thin cardboard
- scissors
- tape
- thread
- pencil
- table

**What to do:**

**1** Draw a kite shape about 8 cm (3 in.) long on the colored cardboard and cut it out. Tape a paper clip in the center.

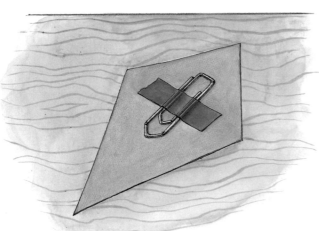

**2** Cut a piece of string about 30 cm (12 in.) long. Tie one end to the paper clip, then thread through the cardboard. Tape the other end to the table.

**3** Bring the magnet near the kite from above.

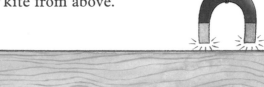

**What happens?**
The kite rises and follows the movements of the magnet.

**Why?**
The magnetic force of the magnet is stronger than the force of gravity that pulls the kite towards the table.

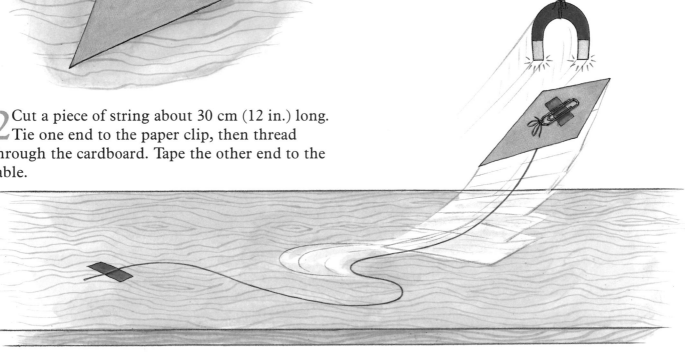

## LET'S GO FISHING!

**You need:**
- scraps of colored plastic
- paper clips
- little stick
- thread
- horseshoe magnet
- large bowl
- water
- scissors

**What to do:**

1 Cut the plastic into some fish shapes.

2 Put a paper clip on the mouth of each fish.

3 Tie the magnet onto the stick with the string. This will be your fishing rod.

4 Fill the bowl with water and put the fish in it.

5 Lower the magnet into the water without touching the fish.

**What happens?**
The fish rise up towards the magnet, as if they are going for the bait!

**Why?**
The magnet exerts a force greater than the gravity that pulls the fish towards the bottom of the bowl.

## Scrap iron for recycling

When buildings or large items of machinery have been demolished, giant magnets are used to separate scrap iron and steel from other metals for recycling. These magnets are powered by electricity and are called electromagnets.

# The force of magnetism can overcome the force of gravity.

# Magnetism and electricity

At one time it was believed that magnetism and electricity were two separate phenomena. But at the beginning of the eighteenth century, the Dutch physicist Hans Oersted and the French scientist André Ampère proved that there were close links between the two. Modern technology makes good use of electromagnetism in turbines, engines, drills, toys, video and tape recorders, telephones, medical equipment, and lots more. An electricity generator, for instance, can be turned on to provide electricity in an emergency. In the next pages you will discover how it is possible to use electricity to generate magnetism, and learn how to build a small electromagnetic motor.

# Is magnetic force produced only by magnets?

## ELECTROMAGNETIC CURRENT

**You need:**
- 4.5-volt battery
- copper wire
- piece of cardboard
- scissors
- iron filings

**What to do:**

**1** Ask an adult to make two holes in the cardboard at least 10 cm (4 in.) apart.

**2** Ask an adult to cut a piece of copper wire about 30 cm (12 in.) long. Thread this through the holes in the cardboard. Then wind the ends around the battery contacts.

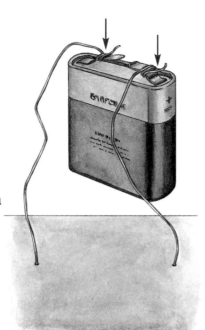

**3** Sprinkle the cardboard with iron filings.

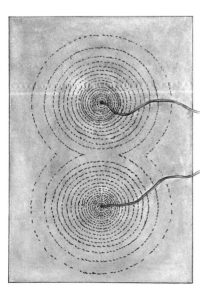

**What happens?**
The iron filings arrange themselves around the copper wire in concentric circles.

**Why?**
The current of electricity generated by the battery, which passes through the copper wire, produces a magnetic field that attracts the iron filings.

**4** Detach one end of the wire from a battery contact.

**5** Move the cardboard to scatter the iron filings.

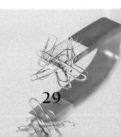

**What happens?**
The iron filings remain scattered on the cardboard in a haphazard way.

**Why?**
The magnetic field generated by the electricity is broken when the flow of electric current is interrupted.

## Fundamental forces

Electricity and magnetism are two different aspects of a unique phenomenon, electromagnetism. It is the electromagnetic force that keeps atoms together in a molecule and keeps solids from falling apart. You can see how important a force it is, considering that everything around us is made up of molecules! The electromagnetic force is one of the four fundamental forces. The other three are the force of gravity, the weak nuclear force, and the strong nuclear force.

The most intense fundamental force is the strong nuclear force, which keeps the protons and neutrons inside the nucleus (the central part) of an atom. Second in intensity is the electromagnetic force, which keeps the atoms in a molecule together. Third in the list of fundamental forces is the weak nuclear force, which keeps together the elementary particles that make up the protons and neutrons in the nucleus. The force of gravity is the weakest on the list – although this force is still strong enough to exert its pull on everything across the whole universe!

## Electrical current can also generate a magnetic field.

# How is an electromagnet made?

## MAGNETISM ON DEMAND

### You need:
- 4.5-volt battery
- little piece of wood
- two metal thumbtacks
- metal paper clip
- copper wire
- large iron nail
- tape
- box of pins
- scissors

### What to do:

1 First, make a switch. Push the two thumbtacks into the wood 2 cm (1 in.) apart. Open up the paper clip into an S shape and thread one end under one of the thumbtacks.

2 Ask an adult to cut a piece of copper wire about 15 cm (6 in.) long. Wind one end around one of the battery contacts. Twist the other end around the thumbtack the paper clip is under.

3 Cut another piece of copper wire about 60–70 cm (24–28 in.) long. Wind the center section of the wire around the nail 10 times.

4 Wind one end of the same wire around the other battery contact. Twist the other end around the second thumbtack.

5 Turn on the switch by using the paper clip to make a connection between the two thumbtacks.

6 Bring the point of the nail near to the pins in the box.

### What happens?
The pins are not drawn by the nail.

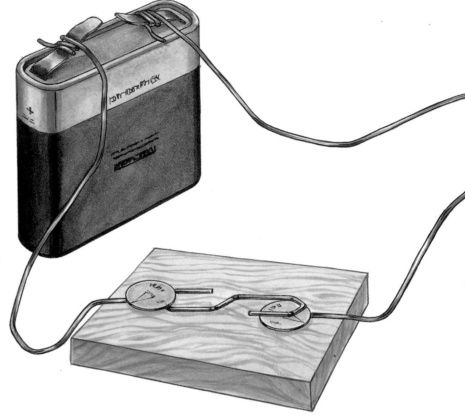

7 Disconnect the switch. Wrap the wire around the nail as many times as possible and as tightly and as close as you can. (It may help to hold the wire in place with tape.) Check to make sure both wires are connected as before.

8 Turn on the switch. Once again bring the point of the nail near the pins.

### What happens?
The nail attracts the pins.

### Why?
The more wire that is wrapped around the nail, the greater the intensity of the magnetic field that is generated. The nail is now a magnet.

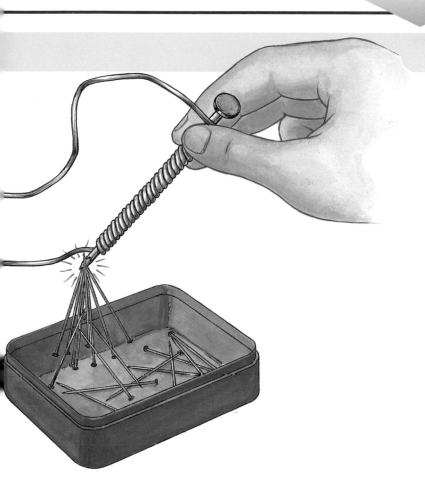

**9** Turn off the switch by moving the paper clip.

**What happens?**
The pins fall back into the box.

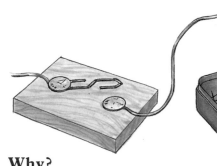

**Why?**
When the flow of electricity generated by the battery is interrupted, the magnetic field disappears, and the iron nail is demagnetized. But if the nail were made of steel, its magnetic power would remain, even in the absence of an electric current.

## The invention of the telegraph

The telegraph, invented by Samuel Morse in 1837, was one of the most revolutionary inventions based on electromagnetism. Morse had the idea of an electric current making an electromagnet move a piece of soft iron to which a writing point was attached. If the current stopped for a short time, the point would stamp a dot on a moving strip of paper. If the flow of electric current stayed off longer, the point would make a dash. Morse worked out a code alphabet (Morse code) in which letters are represented by dots and dashes. His telegraph made it possible to communicate across a greater distance than people could see. And unlike light signals, smoke signals, or flag signaling, the telegraph did not depend on the sender and the receiver being at a certain place at a certain time. So the story of long-distance communication began.

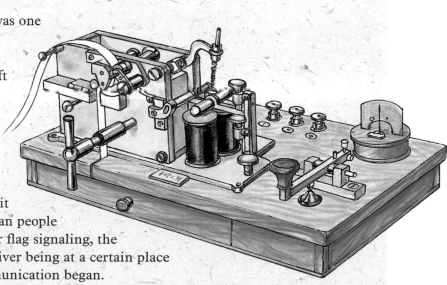

# An electromagnet is a metal object that is magnetized by a current of electricity.

# Can electromagnetic force power a motor?

## A SIMPLE MOTOR

**You need:**
- two bar magnets with the poles marked
- spool
- a few meters (about 10 ft.) of copper wire
- three pieces of insulated wire
- wooden skewer
- two metal thumbtacks
- small piece of wood
- paper clip
- two rubber bands
- four large corks
- two iron washers
- 9-volt battery
- tape

## What to do:

1 Wind the copper wire a number of times around the spool from the bottom to the top. Wind it as tight and as closely as you can, leaving the two ends of the wire free. Hold the wire around the spool with rubber bands.

2 Thread the skewer through the hole in the spool, being careful not to break the copper wire. Thread a washer on either end of the skewer. Thread an end of the wire through each washer.

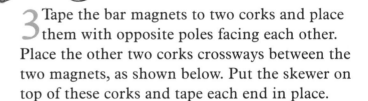

3 Tape the bar magnets to two corks and place them with opposite poles facing each other. Place the other two corks crossways between the two magnets, as shown below. Put the skewer on top of these corks and tape each end in place.

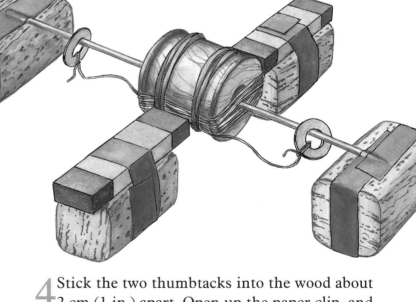

4 Stick the two thumbtacks into the wood about 2 cm (1 in.) apart. Open up the paper clip, and thread one end under one thumbtack so that the clip can be turned to touch the other thumbtack. This will be your switch.

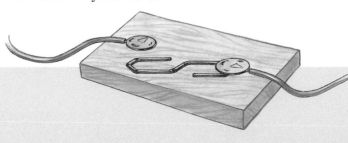

5 Peel off a little of the insulation from the ends of the three pieces of insulated wire. Then run one wire between a battery contact and one washer; one from the other washer to the thumbtack with the paper clip; and one from the other thumbtack to the second battery contact.

6 Turn on the switch by touching the paper clip to the second thumbtack so that the current of electricity can flow through.

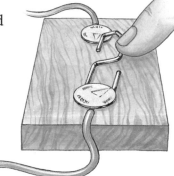

**What happens?**
The spool turns jerkily.

**Why?**
The two magnets generate a magnetic field that runs from the positive pole of one magnet to the negative pole of the other. The electric current creates a second magnetic field around the copper wire. The two fields alternately attract and repel one another, making the spool turn.

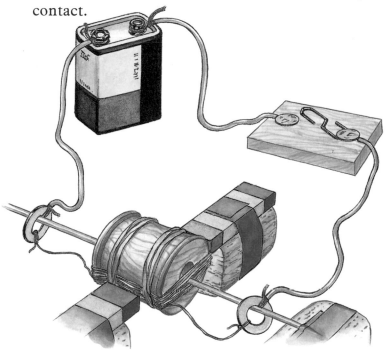

## The electricity of magnetism

The connection between electricity and magnetism allows not only the generation of magnetic fields from an electrical current, but also the other way around – that is, electricity generated by a magnet. This is what happens with the dynamo of a bicycle headlight. The dynamo uses the mechanical energy of a moving wheel to produce the electrical energy necessary for a lightbulb to shine. The movement of the wheel is transmitted through the rotating head of the dynamo. This, in turn, causes a magnet at the center of a thick spring to move. An electric current is created in the wire, due to the magnetic field generated by the moving magnet. This electric current is transmitted to the lightbulb, which lights up. The brightness of the light depends on the speed of the bicycle.

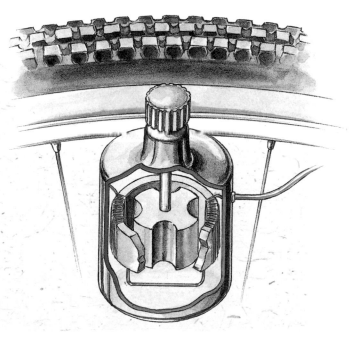

**Electric motors work due to the combination of electricity and magnetism.**

# Does an electromagnet have two poles, like an ordinary magnet?

## ALTERNATING FLOW

### You need:
- large iron nail
- bar magnet with the two poles marked
- 4.5-volt battery
- copper wire
- needle
- piece of cork
- tape
- large bowl
- water
- red paint

### What to do:

1 Magnetize the needle by stroking it 40 times along its length in the same direction with one end of the magnet. Watch the attraction between the south pole of the magnet and the north pole of the needle. Paint the north pole of the needle red.

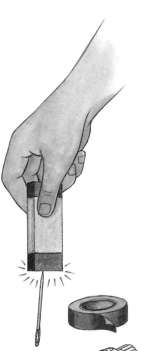

2 Tape the needle to the top of the cork. Fill the bowl with water. Place the cork on the surface of the water.

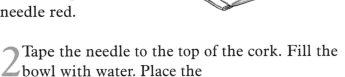

3 Make an electromagnet as explained on pages 30–31.

4 Move the pointed end of the nail towards one end of the magnetized needle, and then the other end.

### What happens?
One end of the needle is attracted by the nail. If this is the colored tip, we know that the point of the nail is the south pole and the other end is the north pole.

5 Detach the copper wire of the electromagnet from the battery and reverse it, attaching each end to the opposite battery contact.

6 Bring the point of the nail near to the end of the needle. At first, the needle will be attracted.

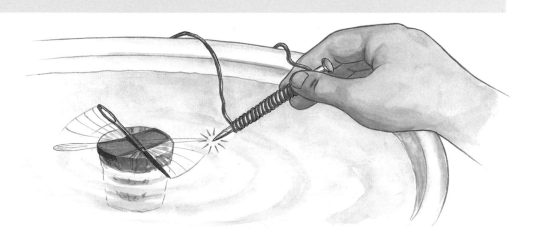

### What happens?
The needle begins to spin.

### Why?
In an electromagnet, the magnetic field is positive or negative, according to the direction in which the current flows. When you reversed the position of the wire, you changed the direction of the electrical flow. As a result of this, you also reversed the poles of the nail.

## Electromagnetic toys
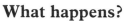
Most moving toys have a little electric motor inside that transforms the electrical energy of a battery into mechanical energy. In these toys there are two electromagnets. One is fixed, and the other is mounted on a rotating axle. The flow of the electrical current creates a magnetic field. The negative pole of the rotating electromagnet moves toward the positive pole of the fixed magnet. The movement of the motor reverses the direction of the current and therefore also the polarity of the magnetic field that it generates. So the rotating electromagnet continually completes the circuit in search of the opposite pole. The rotation of the magnet is transformed into energy to make the toy move.

An electromagnet has two poles, but they are not fixed. They change according to the direction of the electrical current.

## The magnetosphere

This is the name for the volume of space that extends about 500 km (300 mi.) above Earth. In the magnetosphere, charged particles from the Sun become trapped by Earth's magnetic field. The outside of this layer is called the magnetopause. Outside the magnetopause, Earth's magnetic field is not strong enough to trap electrical particles.

## Inverted poles

At present, a compass needle is attracted to Earth's north pole. If Earth's magnetic poles were reversed, the needle would point south. We call this change magnetic inversion. Some polar reversals took place over five hundred thousand years ago, others four thousand or five thousand years ago. One reversal lasted about one thousand years. During each of the reversals, iron-rich minerals were deposited in rocks. As these rocks cooled and solidified, they became magnetized according to the direction of Earth's magnetic field at that time. This is how scientists know that polar reversals have occurred. The age of the rocks tells scientists when the reversals happened.

## Orientation in flight

There have been many theories to explain how migrating birds can travel across vast distances without getting lost. One theory is that birds know how to use Earth's magnetic field to find their way.

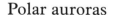

## Polar auroras

Polar auroras are trails of colored light that appear in the night sky near Earth's magnetic poles. They are called aurora borealis in the Arctic and aurora australis in the Antarctic. At about 100 km (60 mi.) above Earth, high-speed charged particles from the Sun, called the solar wind, are pulled by Earth's magnetic field towards the north and south magnetic poles. These particles bombard the gases in Earth's atmosphere, making the gases glow.

## Measure the magnetism

We call the instrument that is used to measure the intensity of magnetic fields a magnetometer. The most widely used is the Hall effect sensor, which measures the intensity of a magnetic field parallel to the surface of Earth. This device, which is related to the transistor, has no moving parts. The presence of a magnetic field changes the direction in which electrons move through the device. The flow of electrons can be measured as an electrical signal.

# Metric Conversion Table

| When you know: | Multiply by: | To find: |
| --- | --- | --- |
| inches (in.) | 2.54 | centimeters (cm) |
| feet (ft.) | 0.3048 | meters (m) |
| yards (yd.) | 0.9144 | meters (m) |
| miles (mi.) | 1.609 | kilometers (km) |
| square feet (sq. ft.) | 0.093 | square meters ($m^2$) |
| square miles (sq. mi.) | 2.59 | square kilometers ($km^2$) |
| acres | 0.405 | hectares (ha) |
| quarts (qt.) | 0.946 | liters (l) |
| gallons (gal.) | 3.785 | liters (l) |
| ounces (oz.) | 28.35 | grams (g) |
| pounds (lb.) | 0.454 | kilograms (kg) |
| tons | 0.907 | metric tons (t) |

To convert degrees Fahrenheit (°F) to degrees Celsius (°C), subtract 32, then multiply by ⅝.

# Glossary

**atom:** the tiniest part of a chemical element that has all the properties of that element

**attraction:** a force that pulls two objects toward each other

**aurora borealis:** colorful bands of flashing lights that sometimes can be seen in the night sky, especially near the Arctic Circle

**compass:** an instrument for finding directions, with a magnetic needle that always points north

**concentric:** having a common center

**diamagnetic:** weakly repelled by a magnet

**dynamo:** a machine that converts the power of a turning wheel into electricity; a generator

**electromagnetism:** magnetism caused by an electric current

**ferromagnetic materials:** substances that are composed of magnetic elements and that are transformed into magnets when they are subjected to a magnetic field that goes in one direction.

**gravity:** the naturally occuring force that attracts objects toward the center of Earth

**magnet:** a piece of metal that attracts iron or steel. Magnets have a north pole and a south pole.

**magnetic field:** the area around a magnet that attracts iron or steel

**magnetic induction:** the process by which an object becomes magnetized when held near a magnet

**magnetic pole:** either of two points on Earth's surface where Earth's magnetic pull is strongest. One of these points is near the North Pole; the other is near the South Pole.

**magnetometer:** an instrument used to measure the intensity of magnetic fields

**magnetosphere:** the volume of space that extends about 500 km (300 mi.) above Earth, in which Earth's magnetic field is strong enough to trap charged particles coming from the Sun

**Morse code:** a way of signaling that uses light or sound in a pattern of dots and dashes to represent letters

**paramagnetic:** weakly pulled toward a magnet

**repel:** to push away

**telegraph:** a device or system for sending messages over long distances, using a code of electrical signals sent by wire or radio

# For Further Reading

Asimov, Isaac. *Asimov's Chronology of Science and Discovery.* New York: HarperCollins, 1994.

DiSpezio, Michael Anthony, and Catherine Leary, ill. *Awesome Experiments in Electricity & Magnetism.* New York: Sterling Publications, 2000.

Fleisher, Paul. *Matter and Energy.* Minneapolis: Lerner Publications Company, 2002.

———. *Waves.* Minneapolis: Lerner Publications Company, 2002.

Fowler, Alan. *What Magnets Can Do.* Danbury, CT: Children's Press, 1995.

Nankivell-Aston, Sally, and Dorothy Jackson. *Science Experiments With Magnets.* Danbury, CT: Franklin Watts, 2000.

Souza, D. M. *Northern Lights.* Minneapolis: Carolrhoda Books, Inc., 1993.

Wood, Robert W. *Who?: Famous Experiments for the Young Scientist.* Philadelphia: Chelsea House Publishers, 1999.

# Websites

*Cool Science,* sponsored by the U.S. Department of Energy
<http://www.fetc.doe.gov/coolscience/index.html>

The Franklin Institute Science Museum online
<http://www.fi.edu/tfi/welcome.html>

NPR's *Sounds Like Science* site
<http://www.npr.org/programs/science>

PBS's *A Science Odyssey* site
<http://www.pbs.org/wgbh/aso>

Science Learning Network
<http://www.sln.org>

Science Museum of Minnesota
<http://www.smm.org>

# Index

# About the Author

Antonella Meiani is an elementary schoolteacher in Milan, Italy. She has written several books and has worked as a consultant for many publishing houses. With this series, she hopes to offer readers the opportunity to have fun with science, to satisfy their curiosity, and to learn essential concepts through the simple joy of experimentation.

# Photo Acknowledgments

The photographs in this book are reproduced by permission of: Galante, D., 5; Archivio IGDA, 7, 14, 27; Cigolini, G., 11; Gellie, Y., 17; Dagli, Orti G., 19; Farabolafoto, 20; Sioen, G., 25; Front cover (bottom) and back cover: Todd Strand/Independent Picture Service.

Illustrations by Pier Giorgio Citterio.